GREAT NORTHERN DIVER
The Loon

◇

by Barbara Juster Esbensen
Illustrated by Mary Barrett Brown

Little, Brown and Company
Boston Toronto London

*This book is lovingly dedicated to Isabel and Alexandra —
the family's newest listeners to the haunting cry of the loon.*
B.J.E.

For Mother and Porter with my love.

My thanks to the Loon Preservation Society in Meredith, New Hampshire,
and especially to Betsy McCoy and Jennifer Levy for their cheerful guidance.
M.B.B.

Text copyright © 1990 by Barbara Juster Esbensen
Illustrations copyright © 1990 by Mary Barrett Brown

First edition

Library of Congress Cataloging-in-Publication Data

Esbensen, Barbara Juster.
    Great northern diver: the loon / by Barbara Juster Esbensen;
illustrated by Mary Barrett Brown. — 1st ed.
        p.   cm.
    Summary: Introduces the elusive loon, one of the most primitive
birds in the United States.
    ISBN 0-316-24954-8
    1. Loons — Juvenile literature.   [1. Loons.]   I. Brown, Mary
Barrett, ill.
QL696.G33E83   1990
598.4'42 — dc20   89-31571
                                                                    CIP
                                                                    AC

10 9 8 7 6 5 4 3 2 1

WOR

Published simultaneously in Canada
by Little, Brown & Company (Canada) Limited

Printed in the United States of America

Loon Call

We hear it —
a soaring shape
clear as glass
or water

An ornament of sound
flung up and up!

It hangs   It breaks
and decorates the northern sky
with echoes

In late April, almost all the ice is gone from this northern lake. Paths of sparkling blue appear between the melting ice floes, and the wild calls of a pair of returning loons echo across the cold sky.

All winter long, the loons live on ice-free ocean coasts hundreds of miles from here. Every spring, they come back to the same northern lake.

When they left this cold lake last fall, they were already wearing their gray-and-white winter plumage. Their winter plumage only changed back to the clear black breeding colors when spring came once again, beckoning them northward.

No other bird has such a unique pattern of black and white. The loon's black wings and back are decorated with a dizzying display of white checks and stripes and dots. Partially circling the neck is an unusual necklace of wavy white lines. The loon's chest and underbelly are snowy white, with no black design at all.

The loon is our most primitive bird. A loonlike fossil tells us that this bird has ancestors that lived millions of years ago. Because loons look so clumsy on land, they were given the name Lumme by the early English speakers. A lumme is a lummox, or an awkward person. A full-grown loon can weigh as much as eleven pounds, though most loons weigh between six and nine pounds, which is very heavy for a bird.

The two returning loons circle the lake at great speed, sounding the high-pitched, crazy laughter of their tremolo call. Their speed and heavy bodies make it impossible for them to drop straight down into the water, feet-first, the way other water birds do when they come in for a landing. Loons must gradually fly lower and lower in order to land.

The pair circles the lake for the second time. Then, just before impact, the two loons paddle their feet furiously in the air and slam onto the surface of the water chest-first, like a seaplane, sending up a wide-splashing spray.

Soon after they arrive, the loons begin a strange performance far
out on the water. Scientists think this may be a way for the birds to
declare their ownership of the territory they have taken as their own.
First the two move slowly toward each other, stretching their long,
arching necks. Swiftly they dip their bills in and out of the cold lake;
over and over their sharp beaks stab the water and quickly flip out again.

The loons stretch their necks until their beaks almost touch. Then, with a sudden wild cry, they both race away, striking the water with powerful beats of their strong wings.

Their chilling calls fill the air as they cut a curving trail in the sparkling water and then rush back to the starting point again. From unseen lakes, ghostly answering cries echo and pulse through the pine forest as more and more loons join in the clamor.

There are many Indian beliefs about the loon's eerie wail. Some say it means that there will be a death soon. Some say the loons are calling for rain. But no one can hear this strange, loud sound without wondering about it.

The loon actually has four distinctly different calls. The TREMOLO call sometimes has as many as eight or ten notes, which pour out into the sky and over the water and seem to come from everywhere at once. Loons use this call to signal alarm, or greeting, or concern about an intruder.

The YODEL sounds a bit like the yodeling sound some humans can make. But it has an untamed wildness to it, and it reminds people of a bloodcurdling shriek or an inhuman, thrilling, chilling call. Often, late at night, whole choruses of loons fly overhead, calling and calling to something unknown.

The loon can also make a sound called a WAIL. It is a sound that many people mistake for the howl of a wolf. Holding its bill nearly shut, the loon forces this call out of its swelling throat.

Loons can HOOT, too. They seem to use this call to talk peacefully among themselves. The KUK-KUK is another kind of "talking" call.

Loon watchers believe that loons mate for life; they have found that when the birds return year after year to the place on the lake that they have chosen for their own, they will not tolerate any intruder. If a third loon should try to enter their territory, the first male will fight him off by standing on the water, sparring and jabbing with his long,

black beak, and flapping his wings furiously to keep his balance. He might even hold the challenger's head underwater until he struggles free and leaves.

A pair may be satisfied to claim a bay on a large lake as its own, but loons will often defend a territory as large as a hundred acres. For this reason, most small lakes have only one nesting pair.

When these two loons are ready to build their big nest, they choose a spot very near the water. A loon's webbed feet are so close to its tail that this water bird cannot walk or run on land. It can move across the ground only by pushing itself along on its chest. The world of water means home and safety to the loon.

Twigs, grasses, soft moss, and cattail stems and leaves are built up by the pair into a nest that is usually about two feet across on the outside and about thirteen inches across on the inside. Sometimes the male loon will build a few extra nests to confuse any predators looking for loon eggs to eat.

For about twenty-nine days, the two parents take turns sitting on the olive-colored egg. Sometimes there are two eggs, but loons almost never lay three. Sudden storms can churn the water to creamy foam and threaten to flood the nest, but the parent will keep the egg dry and warm.

In the shadowy moonlight, a raccoon steals toward the nest. The loon's red eyes are alert, and before the raccoon can dodge out of the way, the bird's fierce beak has darted out. The raccoon shambles away.

Then, one warm afternoon, a small sound comes from the egg. The tiny loon inside is chip-chipping away at the shell. Soon the end of the shell breaks open. Out struggles a bedraggled baby loon, covered with wet black down. Like his parents, he has black feet and a black beak, but he doesn't have their red eyes. His eyes will be dark until he is older.

As soon as the down is dry and fluffy, the chick goes into the water. For the first two months, the parents bring their chick small fish or crayfish to eat. Before giving the food to the baby loon, the parents make it splash around in the water. The baby notices the splashing and sees the tasty food.

The tiny chick gobbles up the food whole and then wants more! Even when it is only a week old, the baby loon can dive and catch its own fish. But just the same, the parents will feed it until it is six weeks old.

The loon parents take good care of their chick. If there is danger from an animal, the parent will hide the baby along the shore. Then the big loon will swim underwater and pop up far out on the lake, calling loudly to take the enemy's attention away from the chick.

For the first week, the chick never goes far from the nest. As it learns to be a better swimmer and diver, it dares to go further away from safety and swims into deeper water.

Baby loons often go for long rides on their parents' backs. The parent sinks low in the water so that the baby can climb on board more easily. Then the big bird raises both wings a little to form a nice cradle for the chick to ride in. When the adult loon has had enough, it sometimes shakes its feathers until the baby falls off. Sometimes the parent just sinks down, down, down, and the baby finds itself floating instead of riding!

Young loons gradually lose their downy look and get their new feathers by the time the leaves begin to turn yellow and red. By then their bills will be bluish-white and their eyes brown. The new plumage will be grayish-brown above, and white below. The young birds won't be black and white with red eyes, like their parents, until they are four years old.

No water bird can swim or dive as well as the loon. Holding their wings tight against their bodies and pushing with their strong, webbed feet, loons can dive as deep as two hundred feet. Their long, webbed toes open wide on the backward push but fold up tightly on the return stroke, helping them to swim fast enough to catch even the swiftest trout. Some loons have stayed underwater for as long as three minutes; once someone saw one stay underwater for ten minutes!

Although a full-grown loon's wingspread is about five feet, it is the smallest wing area of any bird in proportion to its body. This means that the loon has a great deal of trouble getting airborne. It takes off by doing

a half-running, half-flying dash across the lake for as much as a quarter of a mile before its heavy body rises slowly into the air. Sometimes it must make many small circles to get out of a small lake. But once it is in the air, it can fly more than sixty miles an hour.

Fifty years ago, loons were more numerous on northern lakes than they are now. Because they are solitary birds, loons seek isolated places where there are few people. On a hidden lake there is little chance of being disturbed by motorboats coming close to the nest.

Autumn weather comes to this quiet lake in late September. The lake reflects a gray sky, and cold wind scuffs the water. The first golden leaves drift down to the surface. Then more and more begin to fall as the wind rises. The summer birds have left the far northern woods. The trees are bare. It is time for the loons to fly to warmer places once again.

They fly away in the night, in groups of three or four. They fly high and fast, migrating to the ocean coasts, hundreds of miles away. After the loons leave, the cold nights will be silent except for the freezing winds that blow through the forest.

Ice will cover the lake again, and the empty nest on the edge of the water will fill with snow.